Marcia Melissa Bassett Goodwin

Mary Holmes

Pride and Repentance

Marcia Melissa Bassett Goodwin

Mary Holmes
Pride and Repentance

ISBN/EAN: 9783337005009

Printed in Europe, USA, Canada, Australia, Japan

Cover: Foto ©Thomas Meinert / pixelio.de

More available books at **www.hansebooks.com**

THE MINISTER'S CHRISTMAS PRESENT.   (Page 76.)

The
LITTLE
MONITOR
SERIES

CINCINNATI.

R. W. Carroll & Co

MARY HOLMES;

or,

PRIDE AND REPENTANCE.

By Mrs. M. M. B. Goodwin.

CINCINNATI:

R. W. CARROLL & CO., PUBLISHERS,

115 AND 117 WEST FOURTH STREET.

1870.

Mary Holmes; or, Pride and Repentance.

CHAPTER I.

MARY HOLMES was considered a very good little girl. In some respects this was true. She was not saucy or disobedient to her parents, nor was she cross to her little sister, Lois. She helped to pick up chips, drove Brindle from the pasture, gathered wild strawberries for the evening meal, and, when her mother was tired, she often set the table, filled the kettle, and made the tea, afterward washing up the dishes as nicely as need be.

Mary was also a quiet, orderly scholar in the Sunday-school, and invariably had good lessons; but, in connection with her many good qualities, I am sorry to say she had one serious fault. Her love of dress, or pride, threatened to destroy all that was noble or lovable in her nature, just as you have seen a little burdock spring up in the garden and grow till it overshadowed the violets, absorbing the sunlight and dew, while the sweet flower withered and died, and the ugly weed, despised and abhorred, held full possession of the ground.

One Sunday morning farmer Clay came

along, in his big wagon, and took Mr.
and Mrs. Holmes and both the little girls
to church. Mary felt very proud that
morning, for she had a new outfit, a pretty
pink muslin dress, a white hat trimmed
with a wreath of rosebuds, a tiny parasol,
and black lace mits. Lois was also dressed
in equally pretty garments, but little Lois
never seemed to think about her clothes.
Her "primer-book" and "dolly-babies,"
as she called them, were of much more
account than fine clothes, in her esti-
mation.

Mr. Holmes was not a rich man. Indeed, many people will, doubtless, consider
him poor, when they know that his pos-
sessions consisted of only twenty-five acres
of land, a little cottage, a pair of oxen,

and the cow, Brindle.   But poverty is not *always* a lack of money.   In some things this husband and wife were *rich*—they had health, contentment, and that other and higher riches, faith in God.

But I must tell you how the children came to have such costly garments—costly they certainly were—far above the reach of Mr. Holmes's means.

In the city of Philadelphia dwelt a married sister of Mrs. Holmes, a rich and childless woman, who had often begged the parents to give Mary to her, promising to be a mother to her, and to leave her, by will, a large estate; but the parents were too wise to trust their child's future in the hands of this fashionable, worldly woman, and so, failing to get Mary, the

aunt tried to content herself by making
pets of her sister's children, and in sending them nice clothing and pretty toys
and books.

The sermon was over, the ordinance of
the Lord's Supper had been attended to,
and then the Sunday-school classes took
their seats. Just after Mary passed into
the pew and took her place, another little
girl, a stranger, entered and sat down beside her. This little girl, whose name
was Susan White, was dressed in a dark
brown calico dress, faded and patched, and
her shoes were thick calf-skin, well worn
at the toes, while her little gingham sun-
bonnet contrasted strangely with the pretty
flower-wreathed hats of her class-mates.
Although so very poor, Susan's clothing

was scrupulously clean, and her hair was nicely combed.

Now, I am sorry to say that, when Mary saw her enter the class, she curled her lip and tossed her head in a way to make Susan feel very uncomfortable; and when she sat down, Mary drew her dress aside, and whispered, "I don't think you are dressed nice—I wish you'd move along, I don't want to sit beside a girl that wears patches;" and she glanced scornfully at Susan's dress, showing, by her looks and behaviour, that she considered herself quite superior, on account of her fine clothes; forgetting that if she had had no rich aunt to give them to her, she, too, might have been compelled to wear faded calico, for, well as he loved his children,· Mr.

Holmes was too poor to buy them fine garments.

Susan moved away as far as possible, and the teacher just then commenced hearing the verses. Susan had a long Bible lesson, learned perfectly, and when the teacher praised her, she was happy, in spite of Mary's unkindness.

Mary's lesson was not nearly as long, and though she recited it without a mistake, there was a jealous pang in her heart, that a girl in a patched dress should have excelled her in the number of verses. She failed to understand the *first verse*, otherwise it would have been a severe rebuke to her. That verse was—

"Hear ye, and give ear; be not proud: for the Lord hath spoken."

Lucy had often been reproved for her pride. It was a source of anxiety to her parents. Once, when she had expressed her feelings in a very emphatic manner, her mother had kept her in the house until she could repeat the following poem:

THE SILK-WORM'S WILL.

"On a plain rush hurdle a silk-worm lay,
When a proud young princess came that way:
The haughty child of a human king
Threw a side-long glance at the humble thing,
That received with silent gratitude
From the mulberry leaf her simple food,
And shrank, half in scorn and half disgust,
Away from her sister, child of dust;
Declaring she never yet could see
Why a reptile form like this should be;
And that she was not made with nerves so firm,
As calmly to stand by a 'crawling worm!'

"With mute forbearance the silk-worm took
The taunting words and the spurning look,
Alike a stranger to self and pride,
She'd no disquiet from aught beside;
And lived of a meekness and peace possessed,
Which these debar from the human breast;
She only wished, for such harsh abuse,
To find some way to become of use
To the haughty daughter of lordly man;
And thus did she lay a noble plan
To teach her wisdom, and make it plain,
That the humble worm was not made in vain—
A plan so generous, deep, and high,
That to carry it out she must even die.

"'No more,' said she, 'will I drink or eat;
I'll spin and weave me a winding-sheet,
To wrap me up from the sun's clear light,
And hide my form from her wounded sight.
In secret, then, till my end draws nigh,
I'll toil for her; and when I die

I'll leave behind, as a farewell boon,
To the proud young princess, my whole cocoon,
To be reeled and wove to a shining lace,
And hung in a veil o'er her scornful face;
And when she can calmly draw her breath
Through the very threads that have caused my
    death;
When she finds at length she has nerves so firm,
As to wear the shroud of a crawling worm,
May she bear in mind that she walks with pride
In the winding sheet where the silk-worm
    died!'"

The mother hoped this lesson would
cure her child of her folly, and, for a
time, it did seem to made an impression
upon her heart, and she almost ceased
prinking and tossing her head. This
gave her mother great joy, for she knew
that unless this fault was conquered, it

would certainly ruin her child, or, at least, make her very unlovable, and hence her rejoicing when she saw Mary's amendment. But when she witnessed her conduct toward Susan, her heart was grieved, and she sadly pondered upon the subject, resolving, if all other means failed, that she would write to her sister, in Philadelphia, not to send any more clothing for the children, preferring that they should dress even poorer than Susan, to having a spirit of unholy pride engendered in their hearts.

After Sunday-school, Mr. Holmes proposed that they should walk home, across the woods, instead of riding with Mr. Clay, in the jolting wagon. The children were delighted with the proposition, for the path lay through the thick forest, where the most beautiful wild flowers grew, making it like a fairy garden.

When they started, the sun was shining brightly, and they did not notice a dark cloud that hung low in the south-west, otherwise they would have decided to ride. The parents walked slowly along, talking of the sermon, the Sunday-school, and, what more deeply interested them at that time, the proper mode of correcting Mary's pride and growing selfishness.

Suddenly they were startled by a heavy roll of thunder, and great rain-drops began to fall. Mary was the most dismayed of any of the party, not because she was afraid of the lightning, for she did not realize the danger, but because of her clothes—her dress would bear washing, but her pretty hat, with its tiny rose-buds, would surely be ruined—and the tears began to fall, and she begged her father to find a "big tree," but he thought it safest to continue in the path, and, as the rain might not stop till night, to hasten home as soon as possible.

The shower, as it came dashing down, cared very little for false rose-buds—it had been sent to water living flowers, and they smiled and grew brighter as they drank up the pearly drops. The moisture could not wash the color from their bright faces, nor change their beauty and make them look like soiled, dirty rags, as it already had the buds on the children's hats.

Mary's mind was not in a very pleasant state as she picked her way along the edge of the path, which was getting quite muddy. Her dress clung to her, her nice gaiters were thoroughly soaked and out of shape, and her pretty parasol was streaked in a fantastic way where the colors had run together. While she was disconsolately mourning and lamenting over these evils, without minding where she stepped, she went too near a thorn-bush and her wet muslin was caught fast upon the branches. In trying to loosen her dress, her lace mits were torn, her hands shockingly scratched, and she dropped her parasol, Testament, and Sunday-school book upon the ground. The Testament rolled into a little hollow filled with water, and was saturated in a moment, and, upon picking up the books, she disfigured them still more with spots of blood from her thorn-scratched hands. Her father went to her assistance, and her dress was finally released, terribly torn.

The rain ceased just as they emerged from the woods; but Mary was too much grieved over her ruined garments to find any beauty in the rainbow that arched the sky, nor did she have even a pleasant word for Brindle, as they crossed the pasture where she was eating the freshly-washed grass.

At last the pasture bars were nearly reached. Instead of waiting for her father to let them down, Mary ran ahead and undertook to climb over, but the boards were wet and slippery, and she lost her hold and fell, in such a way as to strike her head upon a low stump, and when her father lifted her in his arms her face was so white that he feared she was killed.

Some time elapsed after they had laid her on her little bed, before she showed any signs of life, and when, at last, she opened her eyes, they were wild and bright, and her cheeks were flushed with fever.

Mary was sick for many long weeks, and she had plenty of time to *think*, and, helped by her mother's loving counsel, and by reading, again and again, the story of the meek and lowly Savior, she began to realize how hateful in his sight her conduct had been, and she saw how worse than foolish was the pride which looked to dress—to fine and costly array, which a passing shower or thorn-bush can utterly ruin—as a criterion of real worth.

CHAPTER II.

IT was a warm day, and Mary's chair was drawn before the open door, so that she might look out upon the beautiful landscape. Slowly she was gaining strength, and the roses were coming back to her cheeks. A few more days and she hoped to take her accustomed place in the busy household life, and in her class at the Sunday-school.

As she sat there, watching the blue sky and listening to the rippling of the distant brook that wandered musically over its rocky bed, she heard Lois's voice, and soon caught sight of her, trying to teach her white kitten not to chase the butterflies—birdies, she called them; but kitty was very hard to govern, for no sooner did a bright-winged butterfly sail in sight than off she darted, in spite of Lois's restraining hand. By-and-by she heard a sharp cry of grief, which was presently explained by Lois bringing in the kitten, all dripping wet, and shivering with fear. Poor kit, in jumping after a butterfly, had jumped into the cistern.

"Doing wrong brings bitter punishment, don't it, kitty?" said Mary, wrapping the little thing in her apron, while Lois looked on with tears in her eyes. That Mary's thoughts had gone back to the day when *her* punishment fell upon her was evident, but her heart was comforted with the thought that she should live to redeem her error; and the feeling of gratitude, that God had spared her life, strengthened and deepened.

Presently, upon looking up, the children saw Susan, pausing before the bars, seeming uncertain whether to venture in or to pass on. Mary motioned her to enter, and Lois ran down the path to meet her. Her dress was the same faded calico, but Mary did not feel now like scoffing at her appearance, but was very glad to see her—glad to have an opportunity to tell her how ashamed and sorry she had since become on account of her ill-natured comments.

Susan was ready to forgive her—indeed,

the poor child had never laid up any hardness, and, during Mary's illness, had often wished to visit her, but no company being admitted, she was obliged to wait until she heard of her convalescence.

After Susan had seen all the pretty books and toys belonging to Mary, Lois thought it her turn to entertain the visitor, and she commenced by bringing her the white kitten, who was, by this time, dry and warm, and ready for another frolic. Susan fixed a ball of yarn so that it would not unwind, and, tying it to the door-handle, a few inches from the floor, set it swinging; and so, for the next half-hour, kit had business in plenty without chasing butterflies. Then Lois brought forward a whole regiment of doll-babies—

lame, halt, and blind, if one could judge
from appearances. Miss China-doll had
a fractured skull, and Miss Wax-doll had
both eyes out; Rubber-doll's face had
been washed until she strongly resem-
bled a "contraband," while the two rag-
dolls had only an arm and a half between
them; and if they had ever had any feet,
they had long since "walked off," leaving
the helpless bodies behind; but, in spite
of their disfigurements, these "babies"
were very precious to Lois, and when
Susan offered to repair some of the dam-
ages they had sustained in life's warfare,
she was perfectly happy, and her happi-
ness proved contagious, and the three children worked and chatted, cut and basted,
and, with needles, glue, thread, and cloth,

they finally made quite a respectable family of dolls. So great was the improvement in their looks, that Lois informed her mother, confidentially, that they were "all *dressed* up for Sunday-school."

After the dolls were completed, Susan proposed to go out in the edge of the wood-lot and gather some black raspberries for tea. Mrs. Holmes gladly accepted her offer, as, since Mary's sickness she could get very little time to gather berries, and Lois was too small to trust out alone in the berry-field; she begged so hard, however, to go with Susan, that her mother consented.

The two took their little tin-pails and wended their way through the pasture to the wood-lot. Here they found the bushes covered with the ripened fruit, and Susan soon filled her own pail, and helped Lois until hers, too, was heaped to the brim. As they started for home they passed near a large, dead tree, and Lois, catching hold of Susan's arm, said, in a frightened tone, "What makes *um* buzz so?" Listening for a moment, Susan became convinced that there must be a swarm of bees in the tree, and she quieted Lois's fears, and they proceeded to the house, where they found the table set and the biscuit nicely browned.

Mrs. Holmes looked over a dish of the berries, and then tossed some cold water over them to cool them and take off the dust; then she sprinkled on the sugar, and covered them with cream, and, calling her husband, and fixing Mary's chair at the table, they all sat down to a repast that a king might have envied.

Susan told Mr. Holmes about the tree "that buzzed so," and he was rejoiced to hear that there was, doubtless, a heavy swarm of bees there at work, and he assured the little girl that when fall came, and he cut the tree, she should receive some of the honey.

After tea, Susan took her leave, but it was with the promise that as soon as Mary was well enough, she and Lois were to spend the day with her. Lois, supposing that the white kitten and her several dolls were included in the invitation, went, very gravely, and informed the dolls that if they kept their dresses clean they could "go visiting;" and to puss she gave the more difficult task of refraining from catching the butterflies.

The next morning Mr. Holmes started, before the children were up, for the nearest village, to be gone all day. As he never made these trips without bringing some little present for wife and children, it is not to be wondered at if the clock *was* watched pretty closely to see if it was not *almost* time to *begin* to look for his coming.

In former days, Mary used always to wish for some new article of clothing; but her pride had really been subdued by her long illness and the Bible instruction she had received, and she whispered softly to Lois, that she did hope papa would bring her a Testament, to replace the one ruined by the rain.

"I want a new dolly *to get 'quainted with,*" Lois confidentially answered; then she added, "My dolls are all quite *'spec-table,* but I'd like a *'spectabler* one!"

Brindle had been milked, and the tea-kettle was singing its cheerful song upon the hearth, when the distant sound of wheels was heard, and Lois darted down to the bars, and soon came running back to tell them that Mr. Clay's white-faced horse was coming over the hill. As Mr. Holmes went with Mr. Clay, in the morning, they had no doubt of his return in the same way, and, sure enough, the wagon stopped in front of the bars, and the two men lifted out a box, with the red mark of the express company upon it, then several bundles and a bandbox, and, last of all, a sort of cage, containing six pretty white "bantam" chickens.

Mrs. Holmes did not seem very much surprised at the numerous boxes and bundles, and the children began to suspect that she must have known more about the matter than she had revealed, and while they were wild with delight, she seemed almost sad. The truth was, she dreaded to have the box from Philadelphia opened, lest it should contain such fine garments that Mary's pride, which she was so anxious to see overcome, should be again aroused.

Soon after tea, Mr. Holmes took the hammer and opened the box in which the white chickens were confined, and giving

one pair to each of the children, told them
that the other pair was for Susan; then
he opened the large box, and, sure enough,
it was filled to the brim with pretty and
useful gifts.

The first thing taken out was a doll,
nearly as large as Lois herself, which could
open and shut its eyes, and say mamma,
papa—provided, of course, that Lois pulled
the wires. Next came a bedstead, a bu-
reau, and a rocking-chair for dolly; then
a box, containing her bedclothes and mat-
tress; then a trunk, with her clothing
nicely packed. You may be sure that
Lois cared very little for the remaining
contents of the big box. Taking her
treasure to the far side of the room, she and
the appreciative kitten passed the remain-

der of the evening in a dream of bliss.
After Lois's presents had been taken out,
there came a large package marked with
Mary's name. Upon opening this, it was
found to contain a beautiful shell-work
box, with a silver thimble, a pair of scis-
sors, bodkins, needles, emery-ball, and
every other implement necessary for a
work-box. A large package of books and
several picture-puzzles, a microscope and
portfolio, with a pretty ivory-handled pen,
were also marked " For Mary."

Next came some dark calico and pretty-
figured muslin, for dresses, two hats, trimmed with blue forget-me-nots, and tiny
blue gaiters, nice enough for a fairy.

Mary watched her mother as she took
out the presents, one by one, but there

was none of the old pride in her eye,
though she felt thankful to the kind aunt
who thus remembered them all.

When her mother handed her the cloth
for her dresses, she looked up with a
timid, tearful eye, and said: "Mamma,
Susan is poorer than we are, and she has
no nice dress to wear to church; may I
give her one of these—the blue muslin.
You know that my Bible-lesson, this
morning, read: 'He that giveth to the
poor, lendeth to the Lord.'   And, mamma, if you are willing, I will give her
the blue gaiters and the new hat.   It's
not *easy* to give away these pretty things,
mamma; but I'm trying to love the dear
Savior more than nice clothes, and I mean
to *obey* him, so that when I die, he will
3 F

give me a spotless robe and golden crown. I think I would rather, hereafter, lay up *some* of my *treasures* in heaven, for the rain taught me how easy it was to have earthly treasures destroyed.

Mrs. Holmes gave her consent to Mary's request, without a moment's hesitation; then she opened the bandbox and showed her the old hat, nicely pressed, and plainly but prettily trimmed with blue ribbon. At the same time, her father took from a brown paper parcel three Testaments, one for each of his children, and another for Susan.

There was no happier little girl than Mary when the next morning came and her father yoked his oxen into the hay-cart and told her and Lois to get in if they wished to go down and see Susan. Mrs. Holmes then brought out a little trunk, in which she placed the presents for Susan—all but the bantam chickens, they had a box to themselves—and, amid many cautions not to play too hard, the happy party rode away.

They found the cottage where Susan lived as clean and neat as soap and water could make it, and the little girl herself engaged in weeding out the garden beds. As soon as she saw who her visitors were, she came forward to welcome them, and she then introduced them to her mother, a pale, weakly woman, to whom Susan was gentle and obedient, and an invaluable assistant.

We leave you to imagine the joy that

pervaded the hearts of both mother and child, when they saw the valuable gifts which had been brought for their acceptance.

The day was not entirely spent in play; Susan and Mary learned their verses for Sunday-school, and read two chapters in the Testament, while Susan's mother explained the meaning of such portions as they did not understand. But, while giving instructions to the older girls, little Lois was not forgotten. Cutting paper was, with Mrs. White, quite an art, and so she made Lois a whole menagerie of animals and birds, and, last of all, taking some pasteboard, she cut a doll's cradle, then sewing the pieces with strong thread, and putting gilt paper over the stitches and around the edges, a toy of real beauty and worth was obtained for the gratified little one, who gravely asserted that she should "'*ock white kit to s'eep.*"

At last, just as the sun was setting, Mr. Holmes came for his little girls, and they were quickly lifted into the hay-cart and on their way home.

The next Sunday morning Mary was well enough to go to church. When she saw Susan enter, dressed as neatly as any of her companions, she learned the joy of charity. She realized the truth of that Scripture which says, "It is more blessed to give than to receive;" and, henceforth, there was no danger of her falling back into her old habits of self-pride.

Upon closing the discourse, the preacher,

as usual, invited all of those who desired to obey the Gospel, and become Christians, to come forward; and, while the song of Zion filled the house with "sounding praise," Mary and Susan both passed down the aisle, and stood before the altar.

The song ceased. A deep silence reigned over the congregation, as the minister repeated the Savior's memorable words: "Let the little children come unto me, and forbid them not: for of such is the kingdom of Heaven." Then taking a hand of each, he said: "Little ones, do you believe, with all your hearts, that Jesus Christ is the Son of God, and your Savior?"

As with one voice came the response, "I do!"

Then he told them of the life they would be expected to lead, now that they had taken Christ as their pattern and guide, that they might not only secure their own salvation, but bring honor upon the Church and the cause of the blessed Redeemer.

In a beautiful stream, close beside the church, Susan and Mary entered the baptismal waters. There were few dry eyes, as the waiting friends raised their glad voices in a song of rejoicing; for all who witnessed the scene felt that, though babes, they had become wise; though poor, they were now rich, being heirs of that immortal inheritance promised to obedient believers.

"Blest are the humble souls that see,
 Their emptiness and poverty;
 Treasures of grace to them are given,
 And crown's of joy laid up in Heaven."

As they were returning home, a woman, who had never confessed her sins and accepted Christ, remarked, that according to her belief, such young persons had no business being baptized, "for," said she, "they do n't know what sin means, and, are, therefore, incapable of committing it!"

"O, Mrs. Jones, please do n't say that," cried Mary, with tears in her eyes, "for, when I lay sick so long on my little bed, thinking over all my wickedness—how I had *sometimes* grieved my parents by disobedience, and been cruel to Lois, running away from her, when I knew she would cry — and, above all, harboring such a wicked pride that I would not associate with girls who did not dress nice; when I thought of all these things, and remembered that I was not *too young to die*, I felt that I was not too young *to go to Christ* in his appointed way."

"And I," said Susan, "had great need of the Savior; for, before I had learned of Him—before I knew that He loved the poor as well as the rich, I rebelled against my hard fate; and, thinking no one loved me, and that it was of no use to try to be *good*, I became very wicked. I played in the woods on Lord's-day, stole bird's nests, apples, and cherries; threw stones at innocent cows, quietly feeding in their pasture; chased school-children, with dead snakes, and live mice, and lizards, and laughed at their fright; splashed muddy water upon people's nice clothes whenever I got a chance; in fact, was as sinful as I knew how to be. My conduct caused great grief to my mother, and at last, for her sake, I tried to reform, but instead of looking to Christ, I tried to *make myself good*; but I soon learned, from God's word, that no sinner, old or young, can do this, but that the Savior always stands ready to pardon a penitent believer."

Susan and Mary had no idea that *they* were preaching the Gospel, but, as is often the case, the "foolish were able to confound the wise," for there is a power in the Word of God which takes hold of human souls, no matter who the "preacher" may be. Hence the words of these children so wrought upon this unbelieving woman's heart, that she went home and took down her unused Bible, and, studying it carefully and prayerfully, became convinced that as she was not *too old to die*, she was not *too old to obey the Savior*.

Days and weeks rapidly passed away, and the cool October winds whispered to the flowers and trees that winter was fast approaching. Then the trees decked themselves in a gorgeous robe of gold, garnet, and purple, and the flowers bowed their meek heads, and waited the coming of the frost-king, whose kiss was death. In all these weeks, Susan and Mary had been very happy. Faithful in their attendance at church and Sunday-school, gentle in their manners to their playmates, and deferential to older persons, they had won the love of all. Although never rude or giddy, they were so undeviatingly cheerful, and joined in the innocent amusements of their young companions with such hearty good-will, that becoming a Christian had been divested of much of its gloom and superstitious terror; and their example was soon followed by many of their companions, for, in that way, too, these young Christians preached Jesus.

CHAPTER III.

EVERAL weeks had passed away without any incidents worth recording, when Mary came in one day from the barn, highly elated, and told her mother that she had found a nest containing six eggs—little white eggs—which she was sure belonged to her "banta."

"Perhaps it is Lois's hen's nest," said Mrs. Holmes.

"Well, how am I to find out, mamma? I want so much to know, because—because—"

"Because what?" asked her mother,

anxiously; for Mary's hesitation, and her desire to claim the eggs, looked as though she was again yielding her heart captive to selfishness.

"Please don't ask me," she said, blushing, and turning away.

Just then Lois came in, excitedly calling out, "Mamma! mamma! I v'e found *my* banta's nest—I mean, papa found it, and showed it to me—it's in the hollow stump—come and see!" and Lois breathlessly ran ahead, followed by her mother and Mary.

When they reached the spot, there, sure enough, hid away in the charred hollow of the stump, they found Lois' banta, and very much out of patience she seemed, at their intrusion upon her solitude. She was determined to stick to her nest, and pecked furiously at their hands when they attempted to disturb her.

Mary ran to the house and brought some corn, with which they at last allured her from the nest long enough to count the eggs; when, lo and behold, there were ten. Mary seemed quite as much delighted as Lois herself, at the sight of so many eggs; and then there was a little whispered consultation between the girls, which puzzled Mrs. Holmes exceedingly, for her children were not in the habit of having secrets from her. Still, her heart was very much lightened when she saw that Mary showed no envy at seeing more eggs in this nest than the one in the barn.

Early the next morning Susan came over on purpose to tell the girls that her little banta had eight eggs, and then there was another whispered consultation; but Mrs. Holmes did not trouble herself much about it this time, well knowing that a secret shared by three little folks could not be very dangerous.

Mrs. Holmes tried to persuade the children that it was too late in the season to raise chickens; but they begged so earnestly that their hens might not be disturbed, that she withdrew her objections.

The children still took great interest in the Sunday-school, and their seats were never vacant. The superintendent, one day, proposed that the school should have a picnic, which proposition was, of course, greeted by the scholars with great delight, and, by general consent, the time was set for the following Saturday. The parents seemed to take quite as much interest in the picnic as the children, and entered upon the most wonderful preparations, and so it came to pass, that every little boy's and girl's mother in the neighborhood was soon busy baking cakes, pies, biscuits, and cooking chickens. Long lines were stretched and filled with summer pants, calico dresses, and white aprons, nicely washed and starched, for sensible mothers knew that a clean calico dress was far more suitable than any finer ones for a romp in the woods.

Saturday morning dawned bright and beautiful, and Mrs. Holmes soon had the

4 F

basket packed. First she put in the sandwiches, then the cold chicken and pickles, raspberry pie, sponge cake, and seed-cookies, and then adding a bottle of milk and some cheese, the basket was filled to the brim. Every article it contained had been raised upon the little farm, and was the product of their own labor; but whiter bread or sweeter butter never was seen, while the cake, though made of maple sugar, was as light and delicate as could be desired.

Just as they were ready to start, Mrs. Romaine, the rich Philadelphia aunt, drove up to the door. Mrs. Holmes explained the situation of affairs, and proposed remaining at home, as the children could go with their father. But to this the aunt would not consent, and, remarking that she had no doubt she should enjoy the picnic, donned a large straw hat, and professed herself ready to accompany them.

When they reached the grove they found a large party assembled, and more constantly coming. The children were in great glee, for the minister, assisted by the superintendent, had fixed several grapevine swings for such as loved rough sports; while his wife, and some of the more quietly inclined, prepared to go in search of wintergreens, flowers, lichens, and moss.

Mary, accompanied by her aunt and Susan, joined the latter company, and it was wonderful how fast the time passed, and how happy they all were.

Mrs. Romaine had never lived in the country, and hence she was scarcely prepared for the shining green of the leaves, or the rare pencilings of the forest flowers. Hot-house flowers and plants she had in abundance, and of the most brilliant and gorgeous dyes, but these forest beauties had a delicate tint and perfume entirely unequaled by their bright-hued sisters.

As the pastor's wife was a delicate and feeble woman, she soon grew weary, and, sitting down upon a log beneath a wide-spreading oak, she bade the rest wander at their pleasure; but the children only gathered the closer around her, and begged for a story. So she told them one of Krummacher's little fables, with which the chil-

dren were delighted. This little story is
translated from the German, and I will
try and repeat it here, for the benefit of
my little readers who could not attend the
picnic and hear Mrs. Jason tell it in her
inimitable style:

ERIC AND THERESA.

"Poor, delicate Theresa had been compelled to keep her bed during the finest
part of spring. When she recovered, and
gained new strength, she began to speak
of the flowers, and asked whether they
were blooming as beautiful as the year before; for she was very fond of flowers,
but could not yet go out to gather them.
Then Eric, the brother of the sick girl,
took a basket, and said, secretly, to his

mother, 'I will go and gather the finest flowers of the field for Theresa.'

"He was going out for the first time; for so long as his dear sister had been suffering, he refused to leave her. Now spring appeared to him more charming than ever, for he beheld its beauties with a pious and loving heart.

"The cheerful boy roamed up hill and down dale. The robins were singing, the bees humming, the butterflies fluttering, and the finest flowers were blooming in abundance at his feet. Singing, he went from one hill and from one flower to another. His soul was as pure as the blue azure above him, and his eye as bright as a streamlet springing from a rock.

"At last he had filled his basket with

the most beautiful flowers, and on the top of them lay a wreath of ripe wood-strawberries, strung like garnets, on a blade of grass. Smiling, the happy boy surveyed his full basket, and sat down to rest on the soft moss under the shadow of an oak-tree. Calmly he looked upon the beautiful landscape radiant with the glow of spring, and with a thousand blossoms, and listened to the robins which warbled around him.

"But the boy was weary with joy; the rejoicing of nature and the song of the birds lulled him to repose.

"Thus he lay, beside his filled basket, a living picture of the sensual pleasures—the enjoyment of which had exhausted him—and of their fading.

"The lovely boy slumbered calmly, but meanwhile a thunder-storm approached. Darkly and silently the clouds gathered in the sky, then the lightnings flashed, and the voice of thunder was heard nearer and nearer. Suddenly the wind roared in the branches of the oak, and the boy was terrified, and awoke. On all sides he saw the sky darkened with threatening; no sunbeam brightened the scene. A violent clap of thunder followed. The poor boy was stupefied by the sudden change.

"Son of pleasure, forgetful of life's duties, art thou safer on thy cheerful road?

"Large drops of rain rustled on the foliage of the oak; then the terrified boy grasped his basket and fled.

"The tempest was over him. Rain

and storm increased, the thunder rolled more terribly, the water was streaming from his locks and down his shoulders. He could hardly proceed on his way.

"Suddenly a violent blast of wind caught the basket in the boy's hand, and scattered all his carefully-gathered flowers over the field.

"Then his countenance fell, and with angry mien he hurled the empty basket to the ground. Weeping bitterly, and drenched with rain, he at length reached the house of his parents.

"Wise son of earth, is thy ill-humor, or thy anger, more excusable when one of thy wishes is refused, or a plan miscarries?

"The storm soon exhausted its fury, and

the sky cleared up. The birds began to sing again, and the peasant resumed his labor. The air was purer and cooler, and a sweet calmness prevailed over hill and valley. The refreshed fields smiled with new strength and fragrance, as if nature had but just issued from the hands of the loving Creator, and mankind looked with grateful eyes to the distant clouds which had showered blessings on their fields.

"Storms purify the air, and the blessings of Heaven descend from the dark cloud. Thus, struggles and sufferings ennoble the sons of earth, and make them to bring forth the fruits of righteousness.

"The brightness of the sky again tempted the boy forth. Ashamed of his ill-humor, he went to look for his basket, and to fill it with fresh flowers. He also felt reanimated. The breeze of the cool air, the odor of the fields, the verdant foliage of the trees, the songs of the feathered dwellers of the forest—every thing appeared to him doubly beautiful after the thunder-storm and the refreshing rains; and the consciousness of his foolish and unjust temper made him gentle and more modest.

"The joys of this world require the discipline of hard change to sustain and ennoble them—a proof of their earthly nature.

"He found the basket at the declivity of a hill. The prickly branch of a bramble had caught it up and secured it from the wind. The boy looked thank-

fully at the bush, and disengaged the
basket. But great was his delight and
surprise when he looked around. The
field sparkled like the starry sky. The
rain had brought forth thousands of fresh
flowers, had opened thousands of buds,
and dew-drops sparkled on the leaves.
Eric went about gathering them, busy as
a bee.

"The sun was setting when the boy,
with filled basket, hastened cheerfully
home. How delighted he was with the
treasure of his flowers, and the garland
of his newly-collected strawberries! The
setting sun brightened his countenance on
his way homeward; but his eye was still
brighter when he saw the delight and the
thankfulness of his tender sister.

"'Are not the pleasures which we prepare for others the most beautiful?' said his mother, affectionately."

Just as the story was ended, they heard a horn proclaiming the dinner hour. When they reached the picnic ground, they found the table-cloth spread upon a dry knoll, from which the underbrush and logs had been carefully cleared away, and upon the cloth the contents of the various baskets had been arranged, in the most tasteful and inviting manner.

After thanks, the feast commenced, and when the black ants crawled upon the table-cloth and helped themselves to crumbs of bread and bits of cake, running off with pieces twice as large as themselves, the children thought it great fun, and let them go in peace; and when the honey-bees settled on the pies, and sucked at the lumps of sugar, they only laughed, and wondered if the inhabitants of the forest did not think the picnic made on purpose for them.

Lois, who had finished her dinner, was sitting quietly on the grass beside her mother, when she spied a squirrel, looking from the maple-tree, above them. "O, mamma," she cried, " the 'quirrel thinks he's a Sun'ay-school scholar, and he's come to the picnic;" but, even as she spoke, the squirrel, alarmed at the noise, leaped from branch to branch, and was soon out of sight.

When dinner was over, the children

united in singing such sweet hymns that even the birds hushed their warbling to listen. It was not until the sun warned them, by sending slant beams from low in the west, that he was already on his way to visit the denizens on the other side of the globe, that the baskets were packed and the good-byes spoken.

The next day Mrs. Romaine accompanied the family to church. The sermon was a short but well-digested exposition of the duties of faith, repentance, and obedience, and Mrs. Romaine listened with a new comprehension of the wonders of Christianity. The very simplicity of the speaker, and all absence of cant and self-righteousness, gave a winning grace and power to the words he uttered.

In the city were hundreds of churches, and one of the most fashionable of these she constantly attended; but the organ and rituals, the forms and ceremonies, had never touched her heart as did the simple prayers, the pleasant hymns, and cheerful kindness of this country preacher and his little band of disciples. She went home that day, with the preacher's last words— "It pleased God, by the foolishness of preaching, to save them that believe"— ringing in her ears. Never before had she realized what the word *belief* implied. Like thousands of others, she had given credence to the story of Christ's death, burial, and resurrection, but its influence upon her life, or her motives of action, had not made her a follower of the lowly

Nazarene in any deep or significant sense. She frequented the theater and the ballroom, and worldliness and pride enveloped her like a garment.

"What makes *you* love Jesus?" she asked Mary, as they were sitting in the door-yard, that evening, after tea.

" Why, he loved me first—he died for me, you know! I did not love him once; I wanted my own way; I wanted to think my own thoughts, and not be compelled to do just what the Bible says. But I 'm happier now, much happier, since I learned to love and obey Him, though it is n't the same things that make me happy now.

" I used to be so overjoyed when you sent me beautiful clothes; and when I was dressed in them and went to church and

Sunday-school, instead of paying attention to the sermon and lessons, I was looking round and comparing my clothes with those of other little girls, and saying to myself, no one else dresses so nice; and I whispered this so often to my own heart that I came at last to believe that I was really better than others, because my clothes were finer.

"But while I was recovering from that long illness, of which my mamma has already told you, I studied the Bible a great deal, and it awoke in my heart a desire to be like Jesus. To do this, I saw that I must trample under my feet the barrier of pride and selfishness, which had arisen mountain high, and hid me from the light of his countenance; and, young as I was, I had learned that the first step to a holy life was obedience to the positive commands of the Gospel. Mamma explained all these things to me, just as I am telling them to you, auntie; and I have not forgotten a single word. Every day I think it all over; for Christ says: 'If you love me, you will keep my commandments;' and unless I remember *why* I am to love him, I might become disobedient."

Mrs. Romaine spent much time during her visit in teaching Mary and Susan how to make beautiful articles with the tiny shells which were to be found in abundance along the sandy banks of the river. She also showed them how to make crosses and baskets, picture frames and vases, and

various other fancy articles from the lichens, evergreens, and moss which grew in
the woods near by.

To Susan and her mother these instructions proved of great value. Articles of
this kind found a ready sale in the city,
and, by sending them there, they were en-
abled to support themselves, and, in time,
they succeeded in saving enough money to
purchase a cow, of which they stood in
great need, and which contributed greatly
to their comfort.

Three weeks had passed, and the little
girls had been so busily employed that
the "bantas" had been left undisturbed by
visits, save those paid them for the purpose of placing water and food near the
nest, and it was, therefore, a real surprise

when Mary's hen, followed by a brood of six of the smallest and yellowest chicks she had ever seen, came strutting and clucking into the yard; and before night, Lois's hen followed, with ten more chickens of the same sort.

The white kitten was lying in the sunshine; upon opening her eyes, she perceived the yellow balls, and, thinking they were legitimate prey, she made a spring toward them; but the two Mrs. Bantas had no intention of allowing their children to be disposed of in that way; so, spreading their wings and opening their beaks, they drove her quite out of the yard. It was a good lesson, and one that kitty needed, for from that time she was never known to chase a chicken or a bird; and, after a while, when her good behavior had proved her reformation complete, it was no uncommon thing to see the white cat, and the two white hens, with their sixteen chickens, eating from the same dish.

The summer passed, and the October frosts had opened the chestnut burs, and dressed the maples in gorgeous crimson robes, when Mrs. Romaine began to talk of returning to her city home. During the last month of her stay, she had studied the Bible most faithfully, and had more than once resolved to give up all for Christ; but the way looked so rough that she hesitated, and feared to start. One morning Mary was reading, for her Bible lesson, the passage of the Israelites through the Red Sea, when her mother stopped her, and turning to Mrs. Romaine, said: "This wonderful miracle teaches us that, as the waves of the sea were parted for the passage of the Israelites, while guided by a pillar of fire, so now, when the waves of temptation rise high before a believer, he has only to take the Bible, and, like the pillar of fire, it will guide him through the parted waters!"

The next Lord's-day Mrs. Romaine confessed the Savior, and when she took her departure from the little woodland cabin, it was with a light heart; and glowing anticipations of the good she would accomplish for the Master's cause through the medium of her great wealth. She did not forget the friends she left, as was evinced by the reception of a box, which, instead of the usual fine clothing, contained a library for the Sunday-school, a large Bible and hymn-book for the pulpit, and a communion service for the Lord's Table. There were also several pieces of flannel, to be distributed among the poor of the congregation, a warm overcoat for the minister, and a merino dress for his wife.

To Mrs. Holmes she sent the title-deed to the wood-lot adjoining her husband's farm, and to Mr. Holmes money sufficient to purchase a span of horses and stout farm-wagon.

*   *   *   *   *   *

It was the week before Christmas. Snow, sufficient to make pretty fair sleighing, had fallen. Mr. Holmes harnessed his horses and prepared to go to town, which, as already stated, was ten miles away. Just as he was putting on his overcoat, Mary brought a basket containing eight white chickens, four from Lois's flock and the same number from her own, with the request that he would sell them. He looked a little surprised, but, without asking any questions, took the basket and placed it in his sled, and drove off. Just as he came in front of Susan's home, she ran to the gate and handed him another basket, containing four of her own chickens, which she desired him to sell.

After handing Mr. Holmes the basket, Susan did not return to the house, but went to spend the day with Mary and

Lois. The children held many whispered consultations, which would, perhaps, have excited Mrs. Holmes's curiosity, had she not already heard Lois rehearsing to her white kitten a detail of their plans for the coming Christmas. So, when Mr. Holmes returned and handed each of the girls two dollars, the amount received for their chickens, she asked no questions and expressed no surprise that they did not consult her as to its disposal.

The day before Christmas, Mary, Susan, and Lois paid a visit to the minister. The two oldest girls had made a nice shell box, and when they handed it to him, it contained three silver dollars, their and Lois's united Christmas-gift to him. They also handed him three other dollars, which, as they told him, they wished used for missionary purposes.

The minister was a poor man, his salary being small. That very day his good wife had informed him that the bottom of the flour barrel was in sight; and, upon looking into the state of his finances, he found his purse as empty as the barrel. I shall leave you to imagine his feelings when these children presented their gifts; but I can assure you their names were not forgotten when he breathed his evening prayer.

I have not time to tell you one half the joys that Christmas brought to these little girls. Their parents quite approved of the use they had made of their money, and had arranged a great many surprises for them. Among the rest was the arrival of a box containing books and toys; and, as their aunt had remembered Susan equally with themselves, their joy was complete. Even the white kitten had her share, and rejoiced in a blue ribbon for her neck, and a worsted mouse with which she could play catch-and-shake to her heart's content.

O, little children, will you not learn, as did those young disciples, that charity and love fill the soul with peace and joy? and will you not strive, as they did, to walk in the light of God's holy Word?

THE END.

www.ingramcontent.com/pod-product-compliance
Lightning Source LLC
Chambersburg PA
CBHW030005030726
47499CB00008B/2912

* 9 7 8 3 3 3 7 0 0 5 0 0 9 *